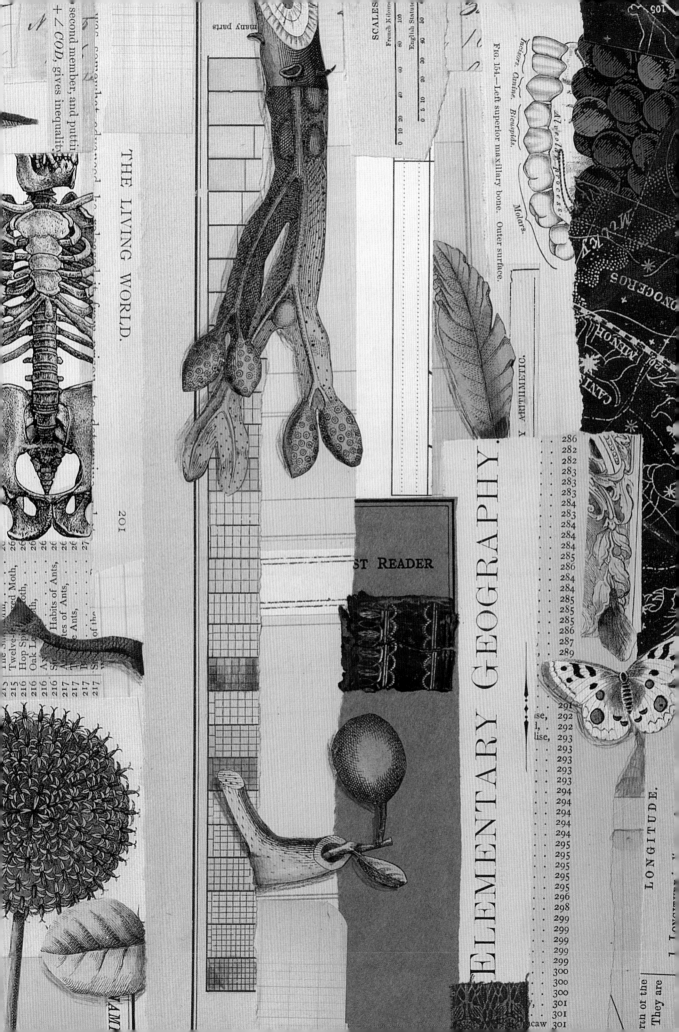

THE RiGHT WORD

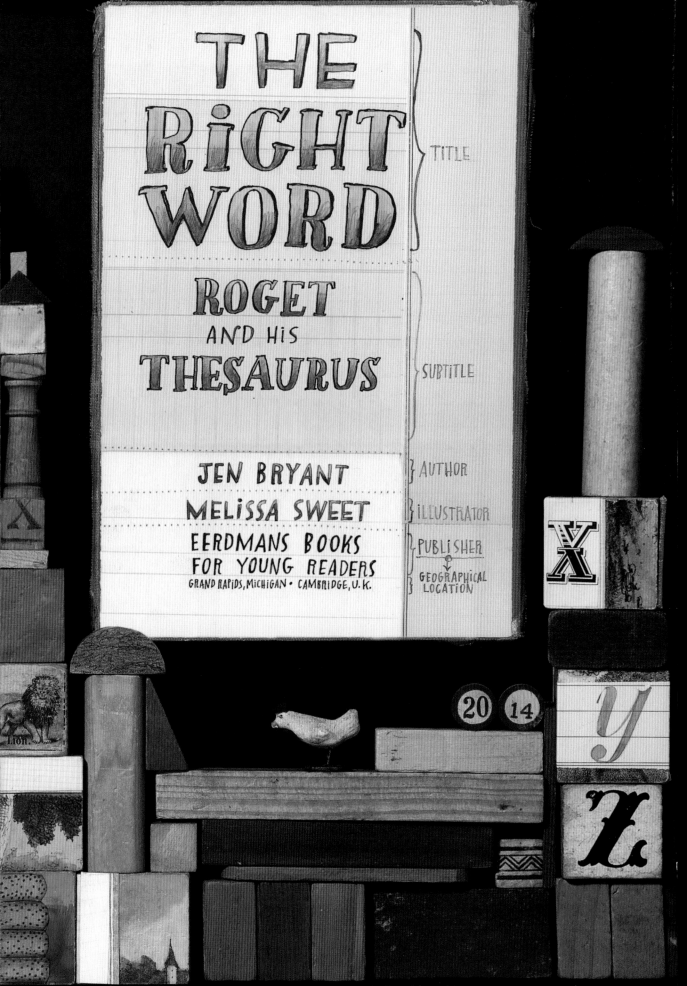

THE RiGHT WORD

TITLE

ROGET AND HiS THESAURUS

SUBTITLE

JEN BRYANT — AUTHOR

MELiSSA SWEET — iLLUSTRATOR

EERDMANS BOOKS FOR YOUNG READERS — PUBLiSHER

GRAND RAPiDS, MiCHiGAN • CAMBRiDGE, U.K. — GEOGRAPHiCAL LOCATION

"**T**HE man is not wholly evil—he has a thesaurus in his cabin."

— J. M. Barrie, author of *Peter Pan*, describing the character Captain Hook

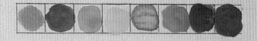

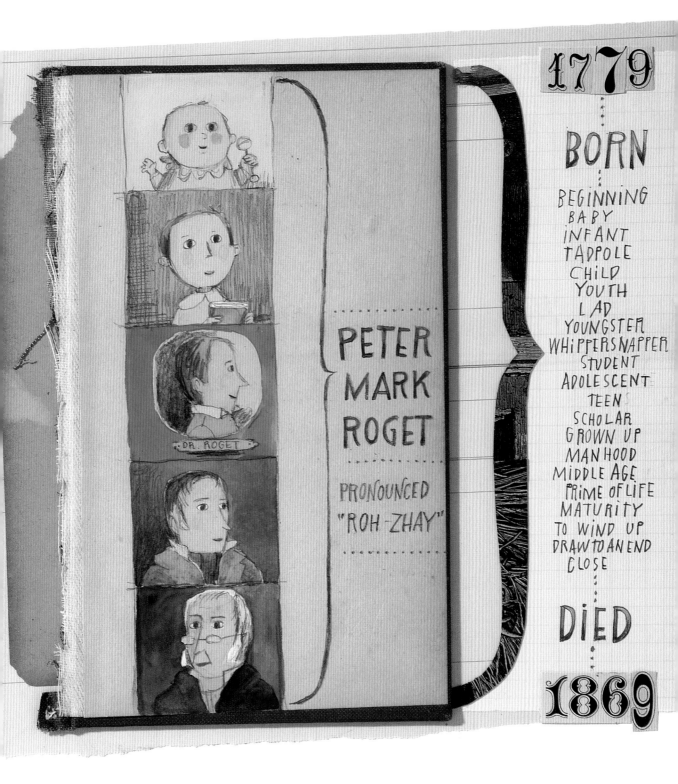

DR. ROGET

PETER
MARK
ROGET

PRONOUNCED
"ROH-ZHAY"

1779

BORN

BEGINNING
BABY
INFANT
TADPOLE
CHILD
YOUTH
LAD
YOUNGSTER
WHIPPERSNAPPER
STUDENT
ADOLESCENT
TEENS
SCHOLAR
GROWN UP
MANHOOD
MIDDLE AGE
PRIME OF LIFE
MATURITY
TO WIND UP
DRAW TO AN END
CLOSE

DIED

1869

1783	DAY	1 2 3 4 5 6	7 8 9 10 11 12 13 14 15 16 17 18 19 20 21 22 23 24
	DATE	SEPTEMBER	OCTOBER
		25 26 27 28 29 30	1 2 3 4 5 6 7 8 9 10 11 12 13 14 15 16 17 18

BERN, SWITZERLAND
⊗ DEPART

GERMANY

HOLLAND

NORTH SEA

LONDON, ENGLAND
⊗ ARRIVE

Peter

snuggled

deeper into

Uncle's lap

as the

carriage

clattered

through

the valleys

of Switzerland.

Baby Annette

slept in

Mother's arms,

a small

pink blossom

against

a wall

of black.

Father wasn't coming back, Peter knew.
Mother's dark dress
and Uncle's sadness proved it.

Years later,
when Peter began his lists,
Father's death came first.

Peter's family moved often, so making friends was difficult.

But books, Peter discovered, were also good friends. There were always plenty of them around, and he never had to leave them behind.

When he was eight, he started to write his own book.
On the cover, he wrote: *Peter, Mark, Roget. His Book.*

But instead of writing stories, he wrote lists.

At first, he made a list of the Latin words
he'd learned from his tutor.
Next to it, he wrote their English meanings.

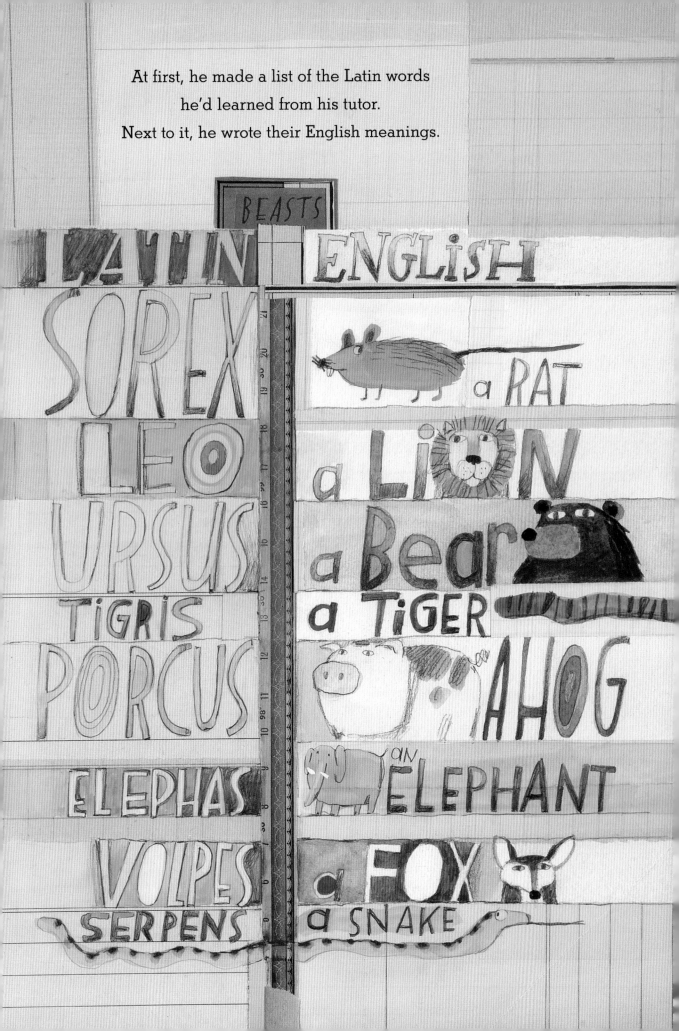

BEASTS

LATIN	ENGLISH
SOREX	a RAT
LEO	a LION
URSUS	a BEAR
TIGRIS	a TIGER
PORCUS	A HOG
ELEPHAS	an ELEPHANT
VOLPES	a FOX
SERPENS	a SNAKE

The lists helped him remember his lessons. They also gave him
something to do when Mother peppered him with questions —

Although, to be honest, Peter thought,
fine wasn't quite the right word.

Every year, Peter added new lists to his book. Some of his favorites were THE FOUR ELEMENTS, OF THE WEATHER, and IN THE GARDEN.

His mother complained that Peter was always scribbling.

SHAPES

CIRCLE HOOP
RING LOOP ORB
NECKLACE LASSO
ELLIPSE
OVAL SQUARE
CONE RECTANGLE
DROP CUBE
GLOBE CYLINDER
EGG
ROUND LIST OF
S AN TRIANGLES
PPLE

1. EQUILATERAL
2. ISOSCELES
3. SCALENE
4. ACUTE
5. RIGHT
6. OBTUSE

NGS
ARE
EN

7. DODECAHEDRON
PYTHAGORAS'S
THEOREM

But Peter's word lists were not just *scribbles*. Words, Peter learned, were powerful things. And when he put them in long, neat rows, he felt as if the world itself clicked into order.

IN THE GARDEN

LATIN	ENGLISH
LATUCA	a LETTUCE
RAPHANUM	a RADISH
LIGNUM	WOOD
POMUM	an APPLE
ARBOR	a TREE

THINGS THAT FLY

Teenage Peter was tall, thin — and very shy. He spent
hours reading science books. He especially liked one
written by Linnaeus, a man who made lists just
like Peter did. Linnaeus put the names of
animals and plants in categories, and
that made nature much easier to study.

SYSTEMA
NATURÆ
CAROLI LINNÆI

EUROPEAN
ROBIN

KINGDOM — ANIMALIA

PHYLUM — CHORDATA

CLASS — AVES

ORDER — PASSERIFORME

FAMILY — MUSCICAPD

GENUS — ERITHACUS

SPECIES — E. rubec

LEAF, STEM

BARB, BRAMBLE,
THORN, THISTLE,
STICK, BUD, FRUIT,
GRASS, GROVE
THICKET
FOREST, SYLVAN,
HEDGE,
SHRUB,
TREE,

TWIG

SONG

ARIA
WARBLE
CHIRP
TRILL
TWITTER
SING
TRUNK, ROOT, TAP ROOT

Just as Linnaeus had wandered through his garden in Sweden, Peter wandered through the London parks, making lists of all the plants and insects.

He preferred to wander alone . . .

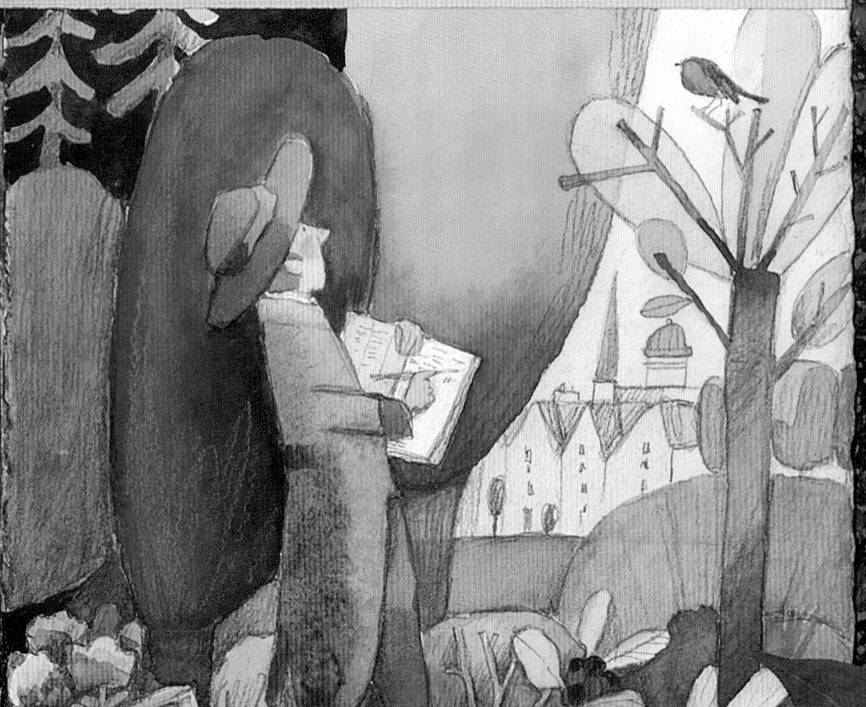

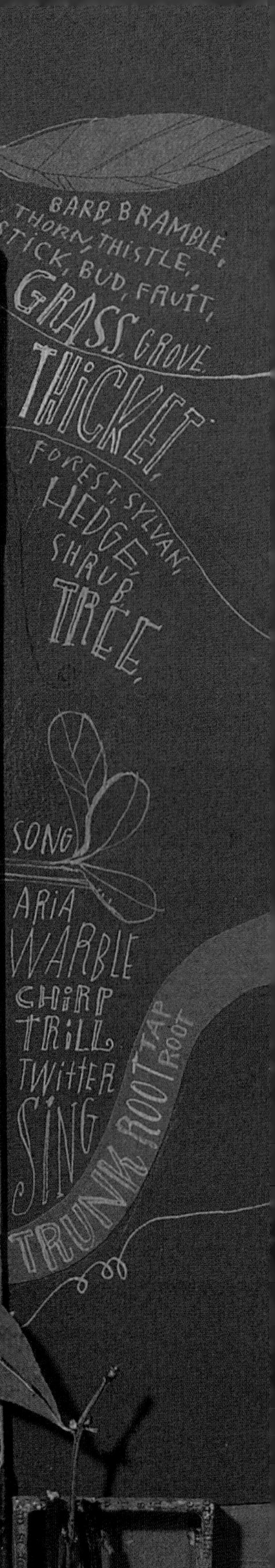

SPRIG

. . . but Mother didn't approve:

Perhaps *worry* wasn't quite the right word.

What was the right word?

Peter began a new list:

How wonderful it felt to find just the right word!

If only all the ideas in the world could be found in one place, then everyone would have one book where they could find the best word, the one that really fit.

Peter carried this idea with him like a secret treasure.

In 1793, the Rogets moved to Edinburgh, Scotland, where Peter entered medical school. For the next five years, Peter studied hard. He was only nineteen when he graduated. His uncle warned him that he was too young to become a doctor.

What could he do in the meantime?
He could teach math, science, and French — he could tutor.

Then he met a wealthy man with two teenage sons . . .

In Paris, Peter and the boys were never short
of things to do or places to go.

They even saw Napoleon lead his troops through the city.

The soldiers marched lockstep in long, orderly
rows, just like the lists in Peter's book.

654. HEALTH.
TO HEAL,
TO CURE,
WELL, HALE,
HARDY.
FRESH AS A
ROSE.

655. DISEASE
SICKNESS.
MALADY.
POX, TO BE
ILL.
THE WORSE
FOR WEAR.

Finally, Peter was old enough to be a doctor. His first job was in Manchester, England. The people who worked in the factories there were poor and often sick. Peter tried his best to keep them healthy.

At night, he worked on his lists.

In 1805, Peter finished his first big book of word lists. It had about one hundred pages, one thousand ideas, and listed more than fifteen thousand words! He kept it on his desk so that he could find just the right word whenever he needed it.

COLLECTIONS
OF
ENGLISH SYNONYMS
CLASSIFIED
AND
ARRANGED

123. NEWNESS.
125. MORNING.

124. OLDNESS

20
86

401

58.
ORDER

PLACE, SYSTEM,
TIDY, UNTANGLED,
APPLE-PIE ORDER.

59.
DISORDER

JUMBLE, MESS,
CHAOS, TOPSY-TURVY,
A PRETTY KETTLE OF FISH.

834
977.

ROYAL SOCIETY

FEAR.

MIDITY
XIETY

NT OF
NFIDENCE)

PPREHENSION,
UGABOO.

COURAGE

RIVE

NERVE
PLUCK,

865. DESIRE
WISH
WANT.

When Peter moved back to London, he joined science societies and attended lectures given by famous thinkers and inventors. Before long, he was asked to give lectures too.

But could he do it? Could shy Peter Roget face a crowded room and talk about what he knew?

Yes, he could.

With his book in hand, Peter spoke concisely, with clarity and conviction!

When he was forty-five years old, Peter married Mary Hobson.
She was cheerful, smart, and pretty. She made Peter laugh.
They had a daughter, Kate, and a son, John.

Peter remained naturally shy, but now he had many friends.

As he grew older, Peter spent less time visiting patients. He
would always be "Doctor Roget," but now he played chess, took
walks, and read books. And, of course, he worked on his lists.

By this time, a few other writers had published their own word lists. These books helped people to speak and to write more politely. Peter read them all.

Kate and John read them too. They thought their father's book was much better.

Peter agreed.

For the next three years, he worked on the book of word lists that he'd written as a young doctor. He made it larger, more organized, and easier to use.

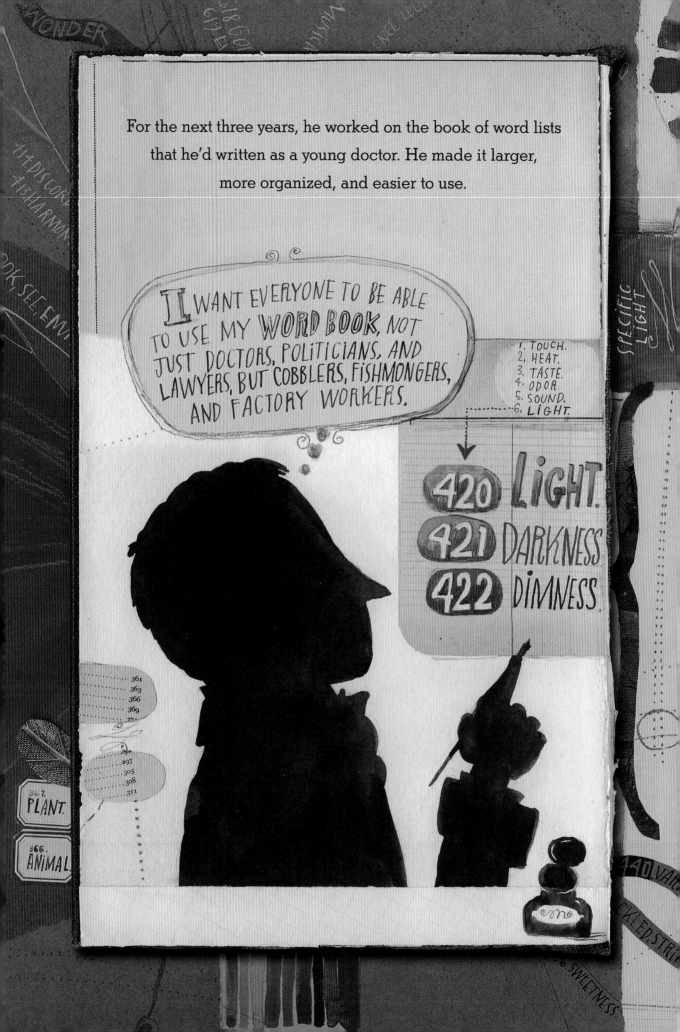

Long ago Peter had discovered the power of words.
Now he believed that everyone should have this power — everyone
should be able to find the right word whenever they needed it.

LIGHT

DARKNESS.

421.

NIGHT GLOOM, DUSK,

DARK as PitcH

SOURCE OF { 423. GLIMMER. SHIMMER. SPARKLE. SHINE.

LIGHT

LUMINARY
SUN
ORB
STAR.

422

411 VISION

DIMNESS.

GLIMMER
OWL'S LIGHT.
MISTY. HAZY
CLOUDY.

COLOR.
GRAY.
REDNESS.
ORANGE.
YELLOWNESS
GREENNESS.
BLUENESS.
PURPLE.
BROWN.

424. SHADE. A SHADOW.

431.

430. WHITENESS.
White AS THE
DRIVEN SNOW.

BLACKNESS.
BLACK AS THUNDER.

SPOTTED DOTTED

In 1852, Roget published his *Thesaurus*, a word that means "treasure house" in Greek. People snatched it from the shelves like a new kind of candy. The first thousand copies sold out quickly.

COMMUNICATION OF IDEAS

551.
553. Record.
554. Recorder.
556. Representation.
557. Painting.
558. Sculpture.
559. Engraving.
560. Artist.
561. Letter.
562. Word.
564. Language.
566. Nomenclature.
567. Phrase.
568. Grammar.
569. Style.

519. Meaning.
518. Intelligibility
520. Equivocalness.
521. Metaphor.
522. Interpretation.
524. Interpreter.
525. Manifestation
527. Information
529. Disclosure.
531. Publication.
532. News.
533. Messenger.
535. Affirmation.
537. Teaching.
540. Teacher.
542. School.

525.
528.
530.
533. Secret
536. Negation.
538. Misteaching.
539. Learning.
541. Learner.

COMMUNICATION...

THIS BOOK IS A MARVEL, A WONDER, A SURPRISE!

ING, audition,
eavesdropping.
ness, nicety, delicacy
acustic organs,
ear-drum, ty
arer, auditor
i, auditory,
o hear, over
give or
e
To
become au
be heard.
Hearing, &
Hark! list
Arrectis

ROGET'S THESAURUS

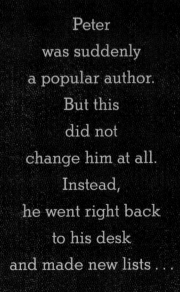

Peter
was suddenly
a popular author.
But this
did not
change him at all.
Instead,
he went right back
to his desk
and made new lists . . .

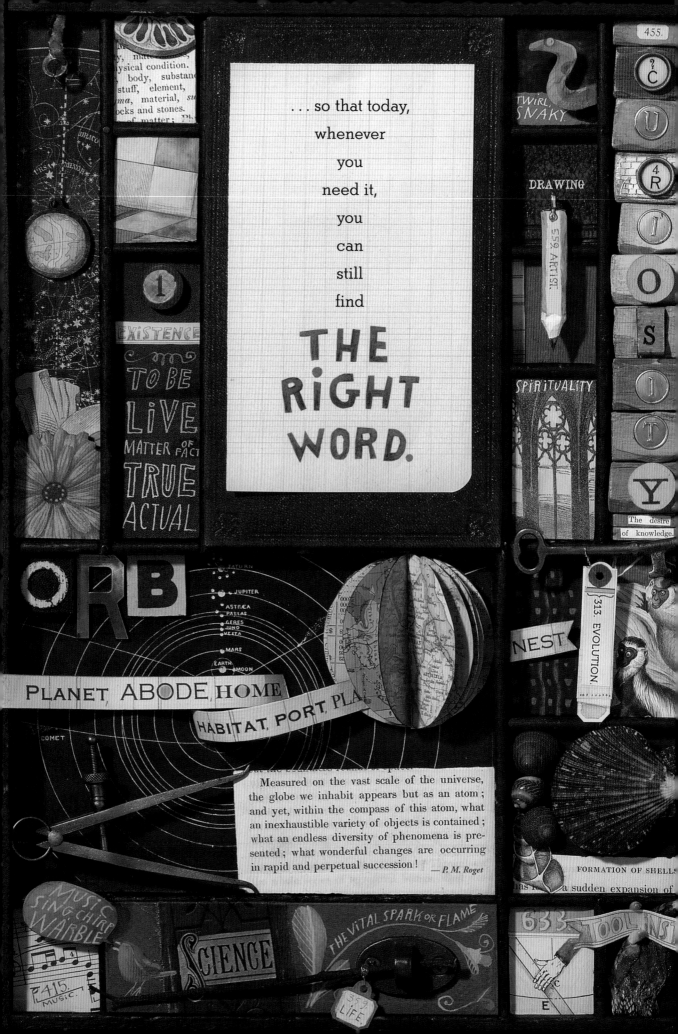

. . . so that today,
whenever
you
need it,
you
can
still
find

THE RiGHT WORD.

TWIRL, SNAKY

DRAWING

559 ARTIST

SPIRITUALITY

455.

C ?

U

R 4

I

O

S

I

T

Y

The desire
of knowledge.

ORB

SATURN
JUPITER
ASTRÆA
PALLAS
CERES
JUNO
VESTA
MARS
EARTH MOON

PLANET, ABODE, HOME

HABITAT, PORT, PLA

COMET

NEST

313. EVOLUTION

Measured on the vast scale of the universe,
the globe we inhabit appears but as an atom;
and yet, within the compass of this atom, what
an inexhaustible variety of objects is contained;
what an endless diversity of phenomena is pre-
sented; what wonderful changes are occurring
in rapid and perpetual succession! — *P. M. Roget*

FORMATION OF SHELLS

has ... a sudden expansion of

MUSIC
SING CHIRP
WARBLE

SCIENCE

THE VITAL SPARK OR FLAME

LIFE

633 TOOL INST

E

P.415.
MUSIC.

EXISTENCE

TO BE
LiVE
MATTER OF FACT
TRUE
ACTUAL

1

LIST of PRINCIPAL EVENTS

The main events in Peter Mark Roget's life appear in black. World events are in red.

1779	Peter Mark Roget is born on January 18 in London, England, to Catherine and Jean Roget.
1779	Peter's father is diagnosed with tuberculosis. In search of a cure, his parents travel to Geneva, where Peter will join them two years later.
1783	The American Revolution ends.
1783	Sister, Annette, is born.
1783	Father, Jean Roget, dies of tuberculosis.
1787	Begins his first notebook: *Peter, Mark, Roget. His Book.*
1793	Fourteen-year-old Peter enters medical school at the University of Edinburgh.
1794	Hester Lynch Piozzi publishes *British Synonymy: Or an Attempt at Regulating the Choice of Words in Familiar Conversation*, one of several precursors to Roget's *Thesaurus*. This book focused on polite speech and social etiquette.
1798	Graduates from medical school.
1798	Edward Jenner discovers vaccine for smallpox.
1799	Volunteers to be a subject in nitrous oxide, or "laughing gas," experiments conducted by inventors Thomas Beddoes and Humphry Davy.
1799	Works with inventor Jeremy Bentham on the development of a "frigidarium" — what will later become known as a refrigerator.
1799	The Rosetta Stone is discovered in Egypt.
1802	Serves as tutor for Burton and Nathaniel Philips as they travel through France and Switzerland. When the Napoleonic Wars begin between France and England in 1803, the three escape through Germany.
1804	Begins first job as a physician in a public infirmary in Manchester, England.
1805	Completes first draft of his word book: *Collections of English Synonyms Classified and Arranged.*
1807	Noah Webster begins compiling a comprehensive dictionary, which he publishes in 1828.
1808	Moves to London. Begins a private physician's practice but also offers his service for free in the poorest parts of the city.
1810	Begins to build his medical practice. Over the next few years he also gives numerous lectures at schools and institutions on a wide range of subjects including chemistry, magnetism, optics, anatomy, and natural philosophy.
1811	Mary Anning (age 12) discovers fossil remains of an ichthyosaur in Dorset, England.
1814	Develops a new slide-rule device. Until the invention of the calculator, the slide rule provided the best way to solve complex division and multiplication problems.
1815	Elected Fellow of the Royal Society, the leading scientific organization in England.

1815	Napoleon Bonaparte is defeated at the Battle of Waterloo and exiled to the British island of Saint Helena.
1816	René Laennec invents the stethoscope.
1817	Roget's friend David Brewster patents the kaleidoscope. Some time later, Roget writes the *Encyclopaedia Britannica* entry about the device.
1818	Mary Shelley publishes *Frankenstein*.
1818	Uncle, Samuel Romilly, dies.
1820	Antarctica is discovered.
1824	Marries Mary Taylor Hobson.
1824	After observing how the spokes of a wheel on a passing carriage appear to bend when seen through vertical window blinds, Peter writes a scientific paper on this optical illusion. This is widely regarded as one of the founding principles of modern cinematography or movies.
1825	Daughter, Catherine ("Kate"), is born.
1827	Elected Secretary of the Royal Society. Also holds membership in the Zoological Society of London, the Royal Entomological Society, the Association for the Advancement of Science, the Royal Geographical Society, the Royal Astronomical Society, and the Society for the Diffusion of Useful Knowledge.
1827	John James Audubon publishes the first volume of *The Birds of America*.
1828	Son, John Lewis, is born.
1833	William Whewell coins the term "scientist."
1833	Wife, Mary, dies after suffering for several years from a painful illness, probably cancer.
1833	Slavery is abolished in the United Kingdom.
1834	Publishes *Animal and Vegetable Physiology Considered with Reference to Natural Theology*, also known as his *Bridgewater Treatise*. This book builds upon his lifelong passion for listing and categorizing plants and animals and establishes him as a leading thinker of his time.
1835	Mother, Catherine, dies.
1837	Princess Victoria becomes Queen of England.
1845	Invents the first pocket chess set.
1852	The first edition of his now-famous *Thesaurus* is published in England. Its full title is *Thesaurus of English Words and Phrases, Classified and Arranged so as to Facilitate the Expression of Ideas and Assist in Literary Composition*. The first printing of a thousand copies sells out quickly. In his lifetime, Roget will oversee twenty-eight additional printings.
1859	Charles Darwin publishes *On the Origin of Species*.
1861	American Civil War begins.
1869	Peter Mark Roget dies on September 12 in West Malvern, England. His son, John Lewis Roget, becomes editor of the *Thesaurus* until 1908, at which time Peter's grandson Samuel takes over. Roget's *Thesaurus* has remained in print continuously to this day.

AUTHOR'S NOTE

590. WRITING.
SCRIBBLE
SCRAWL
SCRATCH
AUTHOR } TO SET ONE'S HAND TO.
COMPOSE

The use of language is not confined to its being the medium through which we communicate our ideas to one another; . . . [it functions] as an instrument of thought; not being merely its vehicle, but giving it wings for flight.

— Peter Mark Roget

Once, on a long drive across Pennsylvania, I found I'd packed an early edition of *Roget's Thesaurus*, mistaking it for the novel I'd planned to read. Resigned, I pored over the meticulously arranged entries, which were not organized alphabetically (like the more abridged, modern versions I'd used), but instead by concepts and ideas. Somehow, the author had catalogued most every word in the English language by its <u>meaning</u>. *Who was this man Roget?* I wondered. *And what compelled him to undertake this immensely difficult task?* These questions were the catalyst for this biography.

When I began to poke around in the real, historical details of Roget's life, I discovered that it encompassed more drama and contradictions than anything I'd written about in fiction. His transient and often lonely childhood, his precocious intellect and nervous habits, his friendships with inventors, his travels, and his medical career — all of these combined to create a broad and fascinating life that I wanted to share with young people.

Beginning at age eight, Roget kept notebooks where he made lists of things that he deemed important or interesting. By the time he was twenty-six years old, he'd completed the first draft of his famous *Thesaurus*, which has stayed in print continuously since 1852. There is hardly a literate child or adult on the planet who has not used *Roget's Thesaurus* or their own language's version of it. The middle-school English student needs a synonym for "nice," the politician wants a more moderate term for "coup," the screen-scanning teen consults the digital lists for an alternative to "break-up." These and millions of other transactions just like them take place daily, and each owes a nod of gratitude to a devoted list-making doctor.

I'm extremely grateful to those who shared their time, expertise, and/or original documents: David Karpeles, founder and CEO of the Karpeles Manuscript Library Museums; David Evans, PhD, professor of psychology and neuroscience, Bucknell University; Karen Drickamer, archival consultant, Special Collections, Musselman Library, Gettysburg College; Diane Gies and Carol Welch, reference librarians, Chester County Library; and also to Alyssa E. Henkin, literary agent, Trident Media; Kathleen Merz, editor, Gayle Brown, art director, and Anita Eerdmans, publisher, at EBYR; and the always astonishing Melissa Sweet.

— *Jen Bryant*

If there was just one word from Roget's *Thesaurus* to describe making this book, it would be *thunderclap*, found under:

872. PRODIGY, *phenomenon, wonder, marvel, miracle, spectacle, sign, portent, thunderclap.*
The proverbial *thunderclap* sounded at the start of my research when I held Roget's original 1805 word book in my hands. On each page Roget had drawn a vertical red line separating a numbered entry from its opposite. There were thousands of words carefully handwritten with nary a cross-out. It was an auspicious beginning.

In the art for *The Right Word*, the Latin lists are from Roget's notebooks. The other lists use only words found in the first edition of Roget's 1852 *Thesaurus*. Roget explained that the words in his *Thesaurus* were arranged "not in alphabetical order as they are in a Dictionary, but according to the ideas which they express." Over time, the *Thesaurus* evolved from classified to alphabetized, but it would be hard to equal how poetic these entries are as one idea leads to another. (On a side note, Roget added an index for easy access. After all, this book was meant for everyone, not just for scientists and scholars.)

The idea of classification and scientific illustration crept into my collages, along with imagery from Roget's *Bridgewater Treatise*, old botanicals, vintage papers, book covers, type drawers, watercolor, and mixed media. The back endpapers list Roget's thousand words with an abbreviated *Plan of Classification*. His original list had 1003 words, but Roget, a stickler for symmetry, created subcategories 450a. ABSENCE OF INTELLECT, 465a. INDISCRIMINATION, and 768a. RELEASE giving him a neat one thousand "ideas."

My great thanks to Dr. David Karpeles for generously sharing his collection of Roget memorabilia; to author Joshua Kendall for speaking with me at length about Roget; and to bookbinder extraordinaire, Athena Moore, for her red leather pieces used in the collages. For the chance to work with Anita Eerdmans, Gayle Brown, Kathleen Merz, and Jen Bryant to bring Roget's story to life, I turn to:

734. PROSPERITY, *good fortune, halcyon, lucky.*
Indeed, *lucky* is the right word.

— *Melissa Sweet*

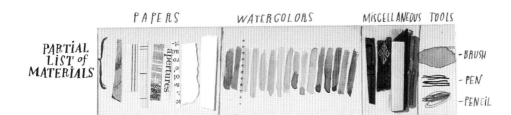

SELECTED BIBLIOGRAPHY

Emblen, D. L. *Peter Mark Roget: The Word and the Man.* London: Longman, 1970.

Kendall, Joshua. *The Man Who Made Lists: Love, Death, Madness, and the Creation of* Roget's Thesaurus. New York: G. P. Putnam's Sons, 2008.

Rennison, Nick. *Peter Mark Roget: The Man Who Became a Book.* Harpenden, Herts: Pocket Essentials, 2007.

Roget, Peter Mark. *Thesaurus of English Words and Phrases, Classified and Arranged so as to Facilitate the Expression of Ideas and Assist in Literary Composition.* London: Longman, Brown, Green, and Longmans, 1852; London: Bloomsbury Books, 1992.

Roget, Peter Mark. *Animal and Vegetable Physiology Considered with Reference to Natural Theology.* Vol. 1, *Bridgewater Treatise V.* London: William Pickering, 1834.

Karpeles Manuscript Library: rain.org/~karpeles/sb.html

The Royal Society: royalsociety.org

FOR FURTHER READING

Brown, Don. *Rare Treasure: Mary Anning and Her Remarkable Discoveries.* Boston: Houghton Mifflin Harcourt, 2003.

Carpenter, Mary Wilson. *Health, Medicine, and Society in Victorian England.* Santa Barbara, CA: Praeger Publishing, 2009.

Ferris, Jeri Chase. *Noah Webster and His Words.* Boston: Houghton Mifflin Harcourt, 2012.

Huxley, Robert, ed. *The Great Naturalists.* London: Thames and Hudson, 2007.

McGinty, Alice B. *Darwin.* Boston: Houghton Mifflin Harcourt, 2009.

SOURCES

"The man is not wholly evil . . ." Barrie, J. M., *Peter Pan and Other Plays*, ed. Peter Hollindale (New York: Oxford University Press, 1995), 136.

"On the vast scale . . ." Roget, Peter Mark, *Animal and Vegetable Physiology Considered with Reference to Natural Theology*, Vol. 1, *Bridgewater Treatise V* (London: William Pickering, 1834), 3.

"The use of language . . ." Roget, Peter Mark, *Thesaurus of English Words and Phrases*, 1st Authorized American Edition (New York: Grosset & Dunlap, 1933), xv.

873. REPUTE.

TO HONOR
DiGNiFY
DEDICATION}...TO EXALT ONE'S HORN.
POSTHUMOUS FAME

For Melissa Sweet, friend and extraordinary
559. ARTIST, *painter, limner, drawer, sketcher, designer, engraver; master.*
— J. B.

To Paul and Patty, my favorite logophiles.
— M. S.

A page from
Roget's original word book

Existence

1

Ens, entity, being, exist^ce

Essence, quintess^ce "quiddess^ce

Nature, thing, substance, course, world, frame, position, constitution

Reality, (v. truth) actual, exist^ce — fact, course of things, under; sun, extant, present

Positive, affirmation, absolute, intrinsic, substantive, inherent

To be, exist, obtain, stand, pass, subsist, prevail, lie — on foot, a; tapis

to constitute, form, compose

State, mode of exist^ce condition, nature, constitut^n habit, Affection, predicament, situat^n posit^n posture, place, contingency

Circumstances, case, plight, train, tune, — point, degree, juncture, conjuncture, pass, emergency, exigency.

— Mode, manner, style, cast, fashion, form, shape, Strain, way, degree. — tenure, terms, tenor, footing, character, capacity

Relation, ~ship affinity, alliance, analogy, filiat^n (v. connect^n

Reference, about, respect^g regard^g concerning, touching, in point of, as to — pertaining to, belong^g applicable to, relatively, according to

Comparable, commensurate, correspondent, accordant

Nonentity, nullity, nihility, nonexist^ce noth^g nought, void, zero, cypher, blank, empty

Unreal, ideal, imaginary, unsubstantial, visionary, fabulous, fictitious, supposititious, absent, shadow; dream, phantom, phantasm

Negation, virtual, extrinsic, potential. adjective

to consist of, scope, habitude, temperament,

incomp^ble incommens^ble —ble, incompatible, irreconcilable, discordant

JEN BRYANT has written numerous books for young readers, including *Georgia's Bones* and *A River of Words*, winner of the Charlotte Zolotow Honor Award (both Eerdmans). Her book *A Splash of Red* (Knopf) received the Schneider Family Book Award and the NCTE Orbis Pictus Award for nonfiction. She lives in Pennsylvania. Visit her website at www.jenbryant.com.

MELISSA SWEET has illustrated a number of books, including *A River of Words* (Eerdmans), a 2009 Caldecott Honor Book, and *A Splash of Red* (Knopf). She also wrote and illustrated *Balloons Over Broadway* (Houghton Mifflin Harcourt), winner of the 2012 Sibert Medal. Melissa lives in Maine. Visit her website at www.melissasweet.net.

Text © 2014 Jen Bryant
Illustrations © 2014 Melissa Sweet

All rights reserved

Published in 2014 by Eerdmans Books for Young Readers,
an imprint of Wm. B. Eerdmans Publishing Co.
2140 Oak Industrial Dr. NE
Grand Rapids, Michigan 49505
P.O. Box 163, Cambridge CB3 9PU U.K.

www.eerdmans.com/youngreaders

Manufactured at Tien Wah Press in Malaysia

15 16 17 18 19 20   9 8 7 6 5 4 3

Library of Congress Cataloging-in-Publication Data

Bryant, Jennifer.
The right word : Roget and his thesaurus / by Jen Bryant; illustrated by Melissa Sweet.
pages cm
ISBN 978-0-8028-5385-1
1. Roget, Peter Mark, 1779-1869 – Juvenile literature. 2. Lexicographers – Great Britain – Biography – Juvenile literature. 3. Philologists – Great Britain – Biography – Juvenile literature. 4. Roget, Peter Mark, 1779-1869. Thesaurus of English words and phrases – Juvenile literature. I. Sweet, Melissa, 1956- illustrator. II. Title.
CT788.R534B79 2014
409.2 – dc23
[B]
2013044348

2014
591. PRINTING.

TO PRINT
PUT TO PRESS
PUBLISH
GET OUT A WO
&c.

Permission is granted by The Karpeles Manuscript Library Museums to reproduce the first page of *Roget's Thesaurus*.

Photography, scanning, and color balancing by Rick Kyle / 5000K Inc.

The illustrations were created with watercolor, collage, and mixed media. The text type was set in Stymie.

THESAURUS OF

ENGLISH WORDS AND PHRASES CLASSIFIED AND ARRANGED

SO AS TO FACILITATE THE EXPRESSION OF IDEAS

AND ASSIST IN LITERARY COMPOSITION

BY PETER MARK ROGET

PLAN OF CLASSIFICATION

CLASS	SECTION	Nos.
I. ABSTRACT RELATIONS	1. EXISTENCE	1 to 8
	2. RELATION	9-24
	3. QUANTITY	25-57
	4. ORDER	58-83
	5. NUMBER	84-105
	6. TIME	106-139
	7. CHANGE	140-152
	8. CAUSATION	153-179
II. SPACE	1. GENERALLY	180-191
	2. DIMENSIONS	192-239
	3. FORM	240-263
	4. MOTION	264-315
III. MATTER	1. GENERALLY	316-320
	2. INORGANIC	321-356
	3. ORGANIC	357-449
IV. INTELLECT	1. FORMATION OF IDEAS	450-515
	2. COMMUNICATION OF IDEAS	516-599
V. VOLITION	1. INDIVIDUAL	600-736
	2. INTERSOCIAL	737-819
VI. AFFECTIONS	1. GENERALLY	820-826
	2. PERSONAL	827-887
	3. SYMPATHETIC	888-921
	4. MORAL	922-975
	5. RELIGIOUS	976-1000

1. EXISTENCE.
3. SUBSTANTIALITY.
5. INTRINSICALITY.
7. STATE.
9. RELATION.
11. CONSANGUINITY.
12. RECIPROCALITY.
13. IDENTITY.
16. UNIFORMITY.
17. SIMILARITY.
19. IMITATION.
21. COPY.
23. AGREEMENT.
25. QUANTITY.
27. EQUALITY.
29. MEAN.
30. COMPENSATION.
31. GREATNESS.
33. SUPERIORITY.
35. INCREASE.
37. ADDITION.
39. ADJUNCT.
41. MIXTURE.
43. JUNCTION.
45. VINCULUM.
46. COHERENCE.
48. COMBINATION.
50. WHOLE.
52. COMPLETENESS.
54. COMPOSITION.
56. COMPONENT.
58. ORDER.
60. ARRANGEMENT.
62. PRECEDENCE.
64. PRECURSOR.
66. BEGINNING.
68. MIDDLE.
69. CONTINUITY.
71. TERM.
72. ASSEMBLAGE.
74. FOCUS.
75. CLASS.
76. INCLUSION.
78. GENERALITY.
80. RULE.
82. CONFORMITY.
84. NUMBER.
85. NUMERATION.
86. LIST.
87. UNITY.
89. DUALITY.
90. DUPLICATION.
92. TRIALITY.
93. TRIPLICATION.
95. QUATERNITY.
96. QUADRUPLICATION.
98. FIVE, &c.
100. PLURALITY.
102. MULTITUDE.
104. REPETITION.
105. INFINITY.
106. DURATION.
108. PERIOD.
110. DIUTURNITY.
112. PERPETUITY.
114. CHRONOMETRY.
116. PRIORITY.
118. PRESENT TIME.
120. SYNCHRONISM.
121. FUTURITY.
123. NEWNESS.
125. MORNING.
127. YOUTH.
129. INFANT.
131. ADOLESCENCE.
132. EARLINESS.
134. OPPORTUNITY.
136. FREQUENCY.
138. PERIODICITY.
140. CHANGE.
141. CESSATION.

144. CONVERSION.
146. REVOLUTION.
147. SUBSTITUTION.
149. MUTABILITY.
151. EVENTUALITY.
153. CAUSE.
155. ATTRIBUTION.
157. POWER.
159. STRENGTH.
161. PRODUCTION.
163. REPRODUCTION.
164. PRODUCER.
166. PATERNITY.
168. PRODUCTIVENESS.
170. AGENCY.
171. ENERGY.

2. INEXISTENCE.
4. UNSUBSTANTIALITY.
6. EXTRINSICALITY.
8. CIRCUMSTANCE.
10. IRRELATION.

14. CONTRARIETY.
15. DIFFERENCE.
18. DISSIMILARITY.
20. VARIATION.
22. PROTOTYPE.
24. DISAGREEMENT.
26. DEGREE.
28. INEQUALITY.

32. SMALLNESS.
34. INFERIORITY.
36. DECREASE.
38. SUBDUCTION.
40. REMAINDER.
42. SIMPLENESS.
44. DISJUNCTION.

47. INCOHERENCE.
49. DECOMPOSITION.
51. PART.
53. INCOMPLETENESS.
55. EXCLUSION.
57. EXTRANEOUSNESS.
59. DISORDER.
61. DERANGEMENT.
63. SEQUENCE.
65. SEQUEL.
67. END.

70. DISCONTINUITY.

73. DISPERSION.

77. EXCLUSION.
79. SPECIALITY.
81. MULTIFORMITY.
83. UNCONFORMITY.

88. ACCOMPANIMENT.

91. BISECTION.

94. TRISECTION.

97. QUADRISECTION.
99. QUINQUESECTION, &c.
101. ZERO.
103. FEWNESS.

107. NEVERNESS.
109. COURSE.
111. TRANSIENTNESS.
113. INSTANTANEITY.
115. ANACHRONISM.
117. POSTERIORITY.
119. DIFFERENT TIME.

122. PRETERITION.
124. OLDNESS.
126. EVENING.
128. AGE.
130. VETERAN.

133. LATENESS.
135. INTEMPESTIVITY.
137. INFREQUENCY.
139. IRREGULARITY.

142. PERMANENCE.
143. CONTINUANCE.
145. REVERSION.

148. INTERCHANGE.
150. IMMUTABILITY.
152. DESTINY.
154. EFFECT.
156. CHANCE.
158. IMPOTENCE.
160. WEAKNESS.
162. DESTRUCTION.

165. DESTROYER.
167. POSTERITY.
169. UNPRODUCTIVENESS.

172. INERTNESS.

173. VIOLENCE.
175. INFLUENCE.
176. TENDENCY.
178. CONCURRENCE.
180. SPACE.
183. SITUATION.
184. LOCATION.
186. PRESENCE.
188. INHABITANT.
190. CONTENTS.
192. SIZE.
194. EXPANSION.
196. DISTANCE.
198. INTERVAL.
200. LENGTH.
202. BREADTH.
204. LAYER.
206. HEIGHT.
208. DEPTH.
210. SUMMIT.
212. VERTICALITY.
214. PENDENCY.
216. PARALLELISM.
218. INVERSION.
220. EXTERIORITY.
222. COVERING.
225. INVESTMENT.
227. CIRCUMJACENCE.

229. OUTLINE.
230. EDGE.
231. CIRCUMSCRIPTION.
232. INCLOSURE.
233. LIMIT.
234. FRONT.
236. LATERALITY.
238. DEXTRALITY.
240. FORM.
242. SYMMETRY.
244. ANGULARITY.
245. CURVATURE.
247. CIRCULARITY.
249. ROTUNDITY.
250. CONVEXITY.

253. SHARPNESS.
255. SMOOTHNESS.
257. NOTCH.
258. FOLD.
259. FURROW.
260. OPENING.
262. PERFORATOR.
264. MOTION.
266. JOURNEY.
268. TRAVELLER.
270. TRANSFERENCE.
271. CARRIER.
272. VEHICLE.
274. VELOCITY.
276. IMPULSE.
278. DIRECTION.
280. PRECESSION.
282. PROGRESSION.
284. PROPULSION.
286. RECESSION.
288. REPULSION.
290. DIVERGENCE.
292. DEPARTURE.
294. EGRESS.
296. EJECTION.
298. EXCRETION.
300. EXTRACTION.
302. PASSAGE.
303. TRANSCURSION.
305. ASCENT.
307. ELEVATION.
309. LEAP.
311. CIRCUITION.
312. ROTATION.
314. OSCILLATION.
315. AGITATION.
316. MATERIALITY.
318. WORLD.
319. GRAVITY.
321. DENSITY.
323. HARDNESS.
325. ELASTICITY.
327. TENACITY.
329. TEXTURE.
330. PULVERULENCE.
331. FRICTION.
332. LIQUIDITY.
335. LIQUEFACTION.
337. WATER.
339. MOISTURE.
341. OCEAN.
343. LAKE.
345. MARSH.
347. STREAM.
348. RIVER.
350. CONDUIT.
352. SEMILIQUIDITY.
354. PULPINESS.
357. ORGANIZATION.

174. MODERATION.
177. LIABILITY.
179. COUNTERACTION.
181. REGION.
182. PLACE.
185. DISPLACEMENT.
187. ABSENCE.
189. ABODE.
191. RECEPTACLE.
193. LITTLENESS.
195. CONTRACTION.
197. NEARNESS.
199. CONTIGUITY.
201. SHORTNESS.
203. NARROWNESS.
205. FILAMENT.
207. LOWNESS.
209. SHALLOWNESS.
211. BASE.
213. HORIZONTALITY.
215. SUPPORT.
217. OBLIQUITY.
219. CROSSING.
221. INTERIORITY.
223. CENTRALITY.
224. LINING.
226. DIVESTMENT.
228. INTERJACENCE.

235. REAR.
237. ANTEPOSITION.
239. SINISTRALITY.
241. AMORPHISM.
243. DISTORTION.
246. STRAIGHTNESS.
248. CONVOLUTION.

251. FLATNESS.
252. CONCAVITY.
254. BLUNTNESS.
256. ROUGHNESS.

261. CLOSURE.
263. STOPPER.
265. QUIESCENCE.
267. NAVIGATION.
269. MARINER.

273. SHIP.
275. SLOWNESS.
277. RECOIL.
279. DEVIATION.
281. SEQUENCE.
283. REGRESSION.
285. TRACTION.
287. APPROACH.
289. ATTRACTION.
291. CONVERGENCE.
293. ARRIVAL.
295. INGRESS.
297. RECEPTION.
299. FOOD.
301. INSERTION.

304. SHORTCOMING.
306. DESCENT.
308. DEPRESSION.
310. PLUNGE.

313. EVOLUTION.

317. IMMATERIALITY.

320. LEVITY.
322. RARITY.
324. SOFTNESS.
326. INELASTICITY.
328. BRITTLENESS.

333. LUBRICATION.
334. GASEITY.
336. VAPORIZATION.
338. AIR.
340. DRYNESS.
342. LAND.
344. PLAIN.
346. ISLAND.
349. WIND.
351. AIR-PIPE.
353. BUBBLE.
355. UNCTUOUSNESS.
356. OIL.
358. INORGANIZATION.

359. LIFE.
364. ANIMALITY.
366. ANIMAL.
368. ZOOLOGY.
370. CICURATION.
372. MANKIND.
373. MAN.
375. SENSIBILITY.
377. PLEASURE.
379. TOUCH.
380. PERCEPTIONS OF TOUCH.
382. HEAT.
384. CALEFACTION.
386. FURNACE.
388. FUEL.
389. THERMOMETER.
390. TASTE.
392. PUNGENCY.
393. CONDIMENT.
394. SAVORINESS.
396. SWEETNESS.
398. ODOUR.
400. FRAGRANCE.
402. SOUND.
404. LOUDNESS.
406. SNAP.
408. RESONANCE.
410. STRIDOR.
411. CRY.
413. HARMONY.
415. MUSIC.
416. MUSICIAN.
417. MUSICAL INSTRUMENTS.
418. HEARING.
420. LIGHT.
423. LUMINARY.
425. TRANSPARENCY.
428. COLOUR.
430. WHITENESS.
432. GRAY.
434. REDNESS.
436. YELLOWNESS.
438. BLUENESS.
440. VARIEGATION.
441. VISION.
444. SPECTATOR.
445. OPTICAL INSTRUMENTS.
446. VISIBILITY.
448. APPEARANCE.
450. INTELLECT.
451. THOUGHT.
453. IDEA.
455. CURIOSITY.
457. ATTENTION.
459. CARE.
461. INQUIRY.
463. EXPERIMENT.
465. DISCRIMINATION.
466. MEASUREMENT.
467. EVIDENCE.

470. POSSIBILITY.
472. PROBABILITY.
474. CERTAINTY.
476. REASONING.
478. DEMONSTRATION.
480. JUDGMENT.
482. OVER-ESTIMATION.
484. BELIEF.
486. CREDULITY.
488. ASSENT.
490. KNOWLEDGE.
492. SCHOLAR.
494. TRUTH.
496. MAXIM.
498. WISDOM.
500. SAGE.
502. SANITY.

360. DEATH.
361. KILLING.
362. CORPSE.
363. INTERMENT.
365. VEGETABILITY.
367. PLANT.
369. BOTANY.
371. AGRICULTURE.
374. WOMAN.
376. INSENSIBILITY.
378. PAIN.

381. NUMBNESS.

383. COLD.
385. FRIGEFACTION.
387. REFRIGERATORY.

391. INSIPIDITY.

395. UNSAVORINESS.
397. SOURNESS.
399. INODOROUSNESS.
401. FETOR.
403. SILENCE.
405. FAINTNESS.
407. ROLL.
409. SIBILATION.

412. ULULATION.
414. DISCORD.

419. DEAFNESS.
421. DARKNESS.
422. DIMNESS.
424. SHADE.
426. OPACITY.
427. SEMITRANSPARENCY.
429. ACHROMATISM.
431. BLACKNESS.
433. BROWN.
435. GREENNESS.
437. PURPLE.
439. ORANGE.

442. BLINDNESS.
443. DIMSIGHTEDNESS.

447. INVISIBILITY.
449. DISAPPEARANCE.
450a. ABSENCE OF INTELLECT.
452. INCOGITANCY.
454. TOPIC.
456. INCURIOSITY.

458. INATTENTION.
460. NEGLECT.
462. ANSWER.
464. COMPARISON.
465a. INDISCRIMINATION.

468. COUNTER-EVIDENCE.
469. QUALIFICATION.

471. IMPOSSIBILITY.
473. IMPROBABILITY.
475. UNCERTAINTY.
477. SOPHISTRY.
479. CONFUTATION.
481. MISJUDGMENT.
483. DEPRECIATION.
485. DOUBT.
487. INCREDULITY.
489. DISSENT.
491. IGNORANCE.
493. IGNORAMUS.
495. ERROR.
497. ABSURDITY.
499. FOLLY.
501. FOOL.
503. INSANITY.

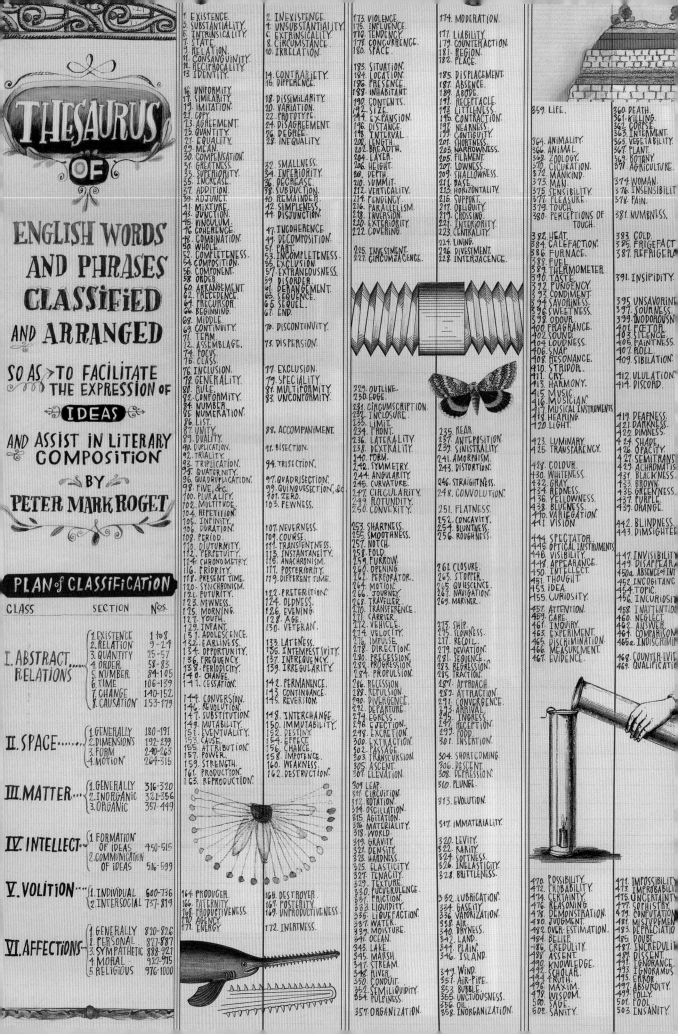